BALLISTIC APOSTOLIC PRAYER

I0181629

McDougal & Associates

Servants of Christ and Stewards of the
Mysteries of God

BALLISTIC APOSTOLIC PRAYER

by

Prophetess Jackie Harewood

BALLISTIC APOSTOLIC PRAYER

Published by:

McDougal & Associates
18896 Greenwell Springs RD
Greenwell Springs, LA 70739
www.thepublishedword.com

McDougal & Associates is dedicated to the spreading of the Gospel of Jesus Christ to as many people as possible in the shortest time possible.

ISBN 978-1-940461-55-7

Printed in the US, the UK and Australia
For Worldwide Distribution

DEDICATION

My dearest **Braylen Landis Coleman**, you truly are an inspiration. As I watch you grow to be a man of integrity, I see in you an intense excitement to learn. It gives me great pleasure to watch your inquisitiveness. You have truly been a gift from the beginning. As a five-year-old author of eight books, you have reignited a passion in me to pick up the pen. So I am dedicating this book to you.

God will established your destiny, so follow the path of righteousness. The results of all our decisions, good and bad, lead us down a path that is unique to our own experiences. Your journey is blessed. The more you love, the more you will be loved. The more you give, the more you will receive. Focus on God and activate His Word, and you will live out your wildest dreams.

Love to you from your Abuelita Jackie

ACKNOWLEDGEMENTS

I wish to personally thank the following for their contributions to this book:

The Holy Spirit for divine inspiration and creativity.

Apostle David Harewood, for being a supportive, inspiring husband. You have demonstrated a love and compassion for me beyond my greatest expectation and are the epitome of what the love of Christ is.

Minister Joachina Julien for helping me with time management.

CONTENTS

And all things, whatsoever ye shall ask in prayer, believing, ye shall receive.

Matthew 21:22

INTRODUCTION

There is a lot of talk these days in the Church about intercessory prayer, but I'm convinced that most of it is just that—talk. It seems to me that few have really captured the revelation of the fullness of this powerful weapon we all have at our disposal.

We have long known that prayer is powerful, but when it is combined with many of the latest revelations on what to pray and how to pray it, our prayers suddenly become something truly awesome, and something very different from the average prayer.

When we are guided by the Holy Spirit and inspired by the examples we find in God's Word, our prayer suddenly becomes a *Ballistic Apostolic Prayer*. What do I mean by that? Well, that's the message of this book, and I trust that it will transform your prayer life, as it has mine, bring you many great victories, and make you a world-changer.

Prophetess Jackie Harewood
Baton Rouge, Louisiana

CHAPTER 1

BALLISTIC APOSTOLIC PRAYER DEFINED

Behold, I will make thee a new sharp threshing instrument having teeth: thou shalt thresh the mountains, and beat them small, and shalt make the hills as chaff.

Isaiah 41:15

The word *ballistic* describes the flight of an object through space. It usually applies to projectiles, like bullets or rockets, that are fired from weapons. *Ballistic,* as it relates to the Spirit realm and leveraged in the natural, is the flight of anointed words through time and space. It provides strategic advantage, giving us the power to act effectively on situations and needs. So, although this word *ballistic* usually applies to bullets, rockets or other weapons, for us, as believers, our projectiles are not bullets but, rather, anointed words spoken from the lips of chosen and prepared vessels.

When Moses died, God said to the children of Israel:

Moses my servant is dead; now therefore arise, go over this Jordan, thou, and all this people, unto the land which I do give to them, even to the children of Israel. Every place that the sole of your foot shall tread upon, that have I given unto you, as I said unto Moses.

Joshua 1:2-3

As we can see from this passage, in the Old Testament, power was in the feet. In the New Testament, however, our power is in our mouth. Our mouth, therefore, is the weapon of the twenty-first century.

When trying to acquire something, like a piece of property, for example, you would find God's Old Testament people marching around it, simply because the Lord had said, *"Every place that the sole of your feet shall tread upon, that have I given unto you."* Today, however, the victory is no longer in our feet. Rather, it is in our mouth. It is the truth that boldly declares: "You shall have what you say." We now possess with our mouth. Every time you release an anointed word from your mouth, you are wielding a dangerous and effective weapon.

The Greek word translated *mouth* in the New Testament is *stoma*, which means "the front edge of a weapon." With this weapon, you can destroy enemies of the human race such as poverty, failure, cancer, diabetes, HIV and many others.

Jesus taught:

Have faith in God. For verily I say unto you, That whosoever shall say unto this mountain, Be thou removed, and be thou cast into the sea; and shall not doubt in his heart, but shall believe that those things which he saith shall come to pass; he shall have whatsoever he saith. Mark 11:22-23

Yes, there is power in your words.

This word *ballistic* comes from a Roman weapon called a *ballista*, which hurled rocks into the air. The name *ballista* was derived from the Greek word for "throw." All truth is parallel. Our missiles are our anointed words which are launched from our mouth and hurled toward the intended enemy.

A ballistic missile is guided only when it is first launched. After that, its flight is subject to the law of gravity. When our anointed words are released into the atmosphere, their flight is subject to the Law of Life in Christ Jesus.

Under the propulsion of the Spirit of life in Christ Jesus, the law that Satan operates under is annihilated.

Paul wrote:

For the law of the Spirit of life in Christ Jesus hath made me free from the law of sin and death.

Romans 8:2

The secret of *Ballistic Apostolic Prayer* is the momentum and the force of our anointed words, enforced by the Law of the Spirit of Life in Christ Jesus. How exciting!

Chapter 2

UNDERSTANDING BALLISTIC PRAYER

No weapon that is formed against thee shall prosper; and every tongue that shall rise against thee in judgment thou shalt condemn. This is the heritage of the servants of the Lord, *and their righteousness is of me, saith the* Lord.   Isaiah 54:17

Anyone given to the ministry of intercession knows that there are special moments in prayer that are met with a certainty of God's immediate intervention. These are breakthrough prayers, and they are dynamic, forceful and perfectly in sync with the purposes of God.

Knowing how and when to apply a specific prayer strategy can make a difference in a situation's outcome. But why are some prayers seemingly more in tune with the will and timing of God than others?

THE RIGHT PRAYER IS IN SYNC WITH GOD

At a prophetic conference, a woman of God approached me who was obviously in pain. "Please pray for my daughter," she cried. "We taught her the Word of God, and she knows the right thing to do, and yet she has walked away from it. She is now living with her boyfriend, and we haven't heard from her in months."

This mother had prayed for her child constantly during this ordeal. Now her request for additional prayer was desperate.

"Lord God," I began, "You are a Father, and so You understand the agony of this mother's heart. I ask You, in the name of Jesus, to bring healing and restoration to this family. Remind this daughter of Your Word. Help her to remember Your goodness."

I sensed the Spirit of the Lord rising up in me, and I could also sense my faith rising. Knowing the authority Jesus has given me, I spoke into the atmosphere, just as if that daughter was standing in front of me at that very moment.

"Devonna," I said, "open your eyes and look. You are in a pigpen. Get up and get out of the pigpen. Come back to your Father's house. Come home! In Jesus' name!"

A month later I received a call from Devonna's mother. She said that when she had gone home from the conference, she received a phone call from her daughter. Devonna said, "I don't know what happened to me! It was as if my eyes were suddenly opened, and I could see again. When it happened, I thought, 'This is a pigpen. I'm going home.' My eyes were opened, and I could see the truth."

Finally, Devonna had acknowledged her blindness in that situation, but what had happened to bring about such a dramatic change? What was different about this prayer from previous prayers? This is a very important point.

Throughout God's Word, He has given us the authority to speak for Him. We are His voice in the Earth today. He has orchestrated a strategic time for our prayers to break through, and, by the power of the Holy Spirit, He will prompt us to pray the right kind of prayer at the right moment. We call this a *kairos* moment.

Kairos is an ancient Greek word meaning "the right or opportune moment (the supreme moment)." The ancient Greeks had two words for time: *chronos* and *kairos*. *Chronos* refers to chronological or sequential time, *Kairos* signifies a time lapse, a moment of indeterminate time in which something happens. *Chronos* is quantitative, but *kairos* has a qualitative and permanent nature to it. Powerful things will happen as we participate with the Lord at specific times.

There is a time warp where we can connect directly into God's *kairos*. This simply means there is a time we can connect to God's right timing, God's fixed or definite time. Simply stated, it is His appointed time to effect dynamic alteration or modification of a given situation.

This opportunity puts you in the portal to inspire immediate change. It opens up a dimension that was not accessible to you before, and new connections are made with angels, to accomplish God's purposes.

In this way, whole networks are established with heavenly hosts that produce new platforms for spiritual ministry. In what were once difficult situations, there are now open doors of opportunity to minister in even greater capacities to the soulish realm of a person. It is this which leads inevitably to their blinders being lifted.

When God sees your faithfulness and your heart to display His will *"on earth as it is in heaven,"* He graces you with a special power to pray.

Nothing goes unnoticed by the Lord when you commit to bringing His will into the earthly realm. He desires that His glory and His Kingdom find expansion in our daily lives, and He desires that the enemy be abated in his potential to effect our lives in any and every way.

God promised through Isaiah:

No weapon that is formed against thee shall prosper; and every tongue that shall rise against thee in judgment thou shalt condemn. This is the heritage of the servants of the LORD, and their righteousness is of me, saith the LORD.   Isaiah 54:17

This word *weapon* is from the Hebrew *kel-ee'*, which means "something prepared, such as artillery." *Artillery* can be defined as "a large but transportable body (physical structure) of forces (strength or energy) equipped (supplied with necessary intention)for war (conflict)."

Our word *formed* here is from the Hebrew word *yatsar,* meaning "squeezing into shape, to mold into a form, especially as a potter. To fashion and form."

GOD FORMED MAN WITH PURPOSE

And God said, Let us make man in our image, after our likeness: and let them have dominion over the fish of the sea, and over the fowl of the air, and over the cattle, and over all the earth, and over every creeping thing that creepeth upon the earth.

So God created man in his own image, in the image of God created he him; male and female created he them.

And God blessed them, and God said unto them, Be fruitful, and multiply, and replenish the earth, and subdue it: and have dominion over the fish of the sea, and over the fowl of the air, and over every

*living thing that moveth upon the
earth.* Genesis 1:26-28

GOD FORMED WOMAN WITH PURPOSE

*And the LORD God said, It is not
good that the man should be alone; I
will make him an help meet for him.
And out of the ground the LORD
God formed every beast of the
field, and every fowl of the air;
and brought them unto Adam to
see what he would call them: and
whatsoever Adam called every living creature, that was the name
thereof. And Adam gave names to
all cattle, and to the fowl of the air,
and to every beast of the field; but
for Adam there was not found an
help meet for him.*

And the LORD God caused a deep sleep to fall upon Adam, and he slept: and he took one of his ribs, and closed up the flesh instead thereof. And the rib, which the LORD God had taken from man, made he a woman, and brought her unto the man. Genesis 2:18-22

According to *Strong's*, this word *made* is from a primitive root meaning "to build, to obtain children, to make, or to repair":

And Adam said, This is now bone of my bones, and flesh of my flesh: she shall be called Woman, because she was taken out of Man. Therefore shall a man leave his father and his mother, and shall cleave unto his wife: and they shall be one flesh.

Genesis 2:23-24

GOD FORMED OTHER CREATURES WITH PURPOSE

And out of the ground the Lord God formed every beast of the field, and every fowl of the air; and brought them unto Adam to see what he would call them: and whatsoever Adam called every living creature, that was the name thereof.

Genesis 2:19

When God said, "*No weapon that is formed against thee shall prosper,*" this word *against* infers "above, over, upon, among, beside, between, beyond the time, and touching." All of these are

Hebrew meanings which are the original intent of the word.

Now let's examine Isaiah 54:17 more closely:

> *No weapon that is formed against thee shall prosper; and every tongue that shall rise against thee in judgment thou shalt condemn. This is the heritage of the servants of the LORD, and their righteousness is of me, saith the LORD.*
>
> Isaiah 54:17

No weapon ... shall prosper: The word *prosper* in Hebrew is *tsaleach,* and it denotes "to push forward, come mightily upon, go over, be profitable or be meet."

Every tongue: This word *tongue*, *lashon* in Hebrew, means "instrument of licking, eating, or speech, a fork of flame, evil speaker or language."

That shall rise against thee in judgment thou shalt condemn: The original intent of the word *rise,* as penned by the author, will astound you. *Rise* is from the Hebrew word *qum*, which denotes "abide, decree, enjoin, hold, perform, pitch, rear up, remain, stand up or stir up."

Against thee: This word *against* is used twice in this verse. The second time it is mentioned it has a different meaning. The first word was *qum*, but the second time it is used, it is the word *eth*, which denotes "nearness, before, by, from and generally with."

In judgement: This is a revealing phrase. The word *judgement* in the original Hebrew denoted "a verdict, especially a sentence or formal decree, a penalty or an ordinance."

Thou shalt condemn: Condemn here is a causative Hebrew word? A causative word is one that produces an effect. This means that *shalt condemn* is an expression causing or forcing a person to perform an action. Not only is *condemn* a causative word; it is a word that denotes "to declare wrong, by implication—to disturb, violate, make trouble, vex, or to deal wickedly." *To declare wrong*, by implication, means

"God brings an incriminating accusation against, above, over, and upon the device sent to you."

This is [our] heritage: This word *heritage,* from *nachalah,* comes from a Hebrew word which means "inherited, occupancy, an heirloom, generally an estate, or possession." *Inherited* here carries a special weight and brings the intent of this word into clearer focus. *Inherited* is "a characteristic occurring among members of a family usually by heredity." *Heredity* is "the biological process whereby genetic factors are transmitted from one generation to the next."

All truth is parallel. Just as we can transfer biological traits, such as the color of our hair and eyes and even diseases, we can also transfer spiritual traits, such as bondages, demonstrative character flaws, behavior traits and blessing. These may be learned and acquired behavior patterns or direct spiritual strengths or weaknesses.

So to make Isaiah 54:17 relevant to ballistic apostolic prayer, we can restate it:

The artillery Satan uses is encased in the shell of discouragement, doubt, fear, condemnation and such like. There are transportable forces equipped to attack you. Satan has always wanted to pervert everything God has created.

We know God's intent:

And God said, Let us make man in our image, after our likeness: and let them have dominion over the fish of the sea, and over the fowl of the air, and over the cattle, and over all the earth, and over every creeping thing that creepeth upon the earth.   Genesis 1:26

But Satan has his own plans. He wants to form and fashion you into *his* nature and character. His aim is to cause circumstances to mold you and distort your witness. He attempts to use circumstances to squeeze you into *his* shape, and the process is very much like a potter working with clay.

Most of the techniques Satan uses will start out with a sweet taste in your mouth and the delusion of freedom.

Once you have taken the bait, however, the taste changes to one of disdain and bondage.

As a believer, no artillery sent against you, over, above, and beside you can have preeminence. Since *against* also means "beyond the time," this suggests that God has placed an expiration date on every prospective attack of the enemy. Now that's good news!

None of the artillery that Satan sends your way will push forward, or break out beyond the limited border God has imposed on its capacity to inflict you. It cannot come mightily upon you, go over you, nor be profitable against you. It simply cannot.

None of the tongues, instruments of speech, forks of flame, or evil speakers that decree, rear up, stand up, or stir up words against or before you that perform a sentence or formal evil decree against you shall be successful. God Himself will condemn it.

Again, *condemn* is a causative word, and a causative word is one that produces an effect. That means that *shalt condemn* is an expression causing or forcing God to perform an action on your behalf. God will disturb, violate, vex, make trouble for and deal wickedly with your every enemy.

God coming to your rescue is your inheritance. *Inheritance* is "the practice of passing on property, titles, debts, rights and obligations upon the death of an individual." What does this mean to us? It means that we inherit the property of the Kingdom of God.

God Himself said it:

Fear not, little flock; for it is your Father's good pleasure to give you the kingdom. Luke 12:32

In the process, we gain the title of royal priesthood and much more:

But ye are a chosen generation, a royal priesthood, an holy nation, a peculiar people; that ye should shew forth the praises of him who hath called you out of darkness into his marvellous light. 1 Peter 2:9

We are sons of God:

But as many as received him, to them gave He power to become

*the sons of God, even to them that
believe on His name.* John 1:12

We have a debt to the world to
herald the Good News, so that some
may come to the saving knowledge of
Christ Jesus.

*For the earnest expectation of the
creature waiteth for the manifesta-
tion of the sons of God.*

Romans 8:19

We have a right to the tree of life,
and we are obligated to enforce the will
of God *"on earth as it is in heaven."*

CHAPTER 3

MAKING STRATEGIC DECLARATIONS

Unto me, who am less than the least of all saints, is this grace given, that I should preach among the Gentiles the unsearchable riches of Christ; and to make all men see what is the fellowship of the mystery, which from the beginning of the world hath been hid in God, who created all things by Jesus Christ: to the intent that now unto the principalities and powers in heavenly places might be known by the church the manifold wisdom of God, according to the eternal purpose which he purposed in Christ Jesus our Lord: in whom we have boldness and access with confidence by the faith of him.

Now unto him that is able to do exceeding abundantly above all that we ask or think, according to the power that worketh in us.

Ephesians 3:8-12 and 20

I became a servant of this Good News through God's kindness freely given to me when his power worked in me.

I am the least of all God's people. Yet, God showed me his kindness by allowing me to spread the Good

News of the immeasurable wealth of Christ to people who are not Jewish. He allowed me to explain the way this mystery works. God, who created all things, kept it hidden in the past. He did this so that now, through the church, he could let the rulers and authorities in heaven know his infinite wisdom.

Ephesians 3:7-10, GW

To the intent that now unto the principalities and powers in heavenly places might be known by the church the manifold wisdom of God. Ephesians 3:10

God established the Church on the Earth to finish the work of putting Satan under His feet. Paul speaks, in Ephesians, of the work and power made available to the Church:

My task is to bring out in the open and make plain what God ... has been doing in secret and behind the scenes all along. Through followers of Jesus like yourselves gathered in churches, this extraordinary plan of God is becoming known and talked about even among the angels!

God can do anything, you know— far more than you could ever imagine or guess or request in your wildest dreams! He does it not by pushing us around but by working within us, his Spirit deeply and gently within us.

Ephesians 3:9-10 and 20-21, MSG

Here Paul indicates that God is going to make known His wisdom through the Church. According to *Strong's*, this word translated *known* comes from the Greek verb *gnoridzo* and means "to certify, to declare, give to understand, to come to know, discover." God will allow the Church to raise the standard by confirming in a formal statement His will.

The echelon of authority is as follows:

1. Believers who have not identified with a specific call from God
2. All the Laity
3. The Minister
4. All the Clergy
5. The Fivefold Ministry (clergy holding a specific office, such as

apostle, prophet, evangelist, pastor, teacher or shepherd

6. Intercessors (a person who intervenes on behalf of another)

Each of these has delegated authority to enforce the will of God. Wherever the Kingdom of God has been established His government and authority prevails, and there is justice, peace and joy in the Spirit. When delegated authority is exercised, righteousness, peace, and joy in the Holy Ghost are the results that are obtained:

For the kingdom of God is not meat and drink; but righteousness, and peace, and joy in the Holy Ghost.

Romans 14:17

Since Christ Himself is the Head over the Church, the human leaders of the Church possess only delegated authority. They merely exercise the authority that Christ has delegated to them:

Now then we are ambassadors for Christ, as though God did beseech you by us: we pray you in Christ's stead, be ye reconciled to God.
                              2 Corinthians 5:20

"To make known" means that God is going to use the Church to make declarations to the demonic rulers and authority. Making declarations is the same as making prophetic proclamations.

According to Zodhiates *Lexical*

Aids to the Old Testament, "The Hebrew word translated *proclaim* is *qara,* which means 'to call out to, call forth, cry unto, invite or preach.' [1] It is usually addressed to a specific recipient and intended to elicit a specific response. Rarely does it refer to a random outcry."

The Greek language has several words that are translated *proclaim.* One of them is *katagello*, which Zodhiates says means "to tell, to declare plainly, openly, or aloud." *Katagello* has the sense of an offer of information or encouragement." [2] We find this word used to describe one of the results of the communion table:

---

1. Spiros Zodhiates, *Lexical Aids to the Old Testament, Hebrew-Greek Key Study Bible* (Chattanooga, TN: AMG Publishers,1984)
2. Ibid

*For as often as you eat this bread
and drink the cup, you proclaim the
Lord's death until He comes.*

1 Corinthians 11:26, RSV

When we partake of the elements of the communion table, we are making an announcement or giving a report about the Lord's death.

According to Zodhiates, another Greek word translated *proclaim* is *kerusso*. A much stronger word, it means "to be a herald." A herald was a public crier who was a speaker of divine truth. The message delivered by the crier was a public and authoritative announcement that demanded compliance. And when you *kerusso* in prayer, you are like a town crier, making an announcement that requires the hearers to comply.

51

TOWN CRIERS

Today public heralds have been replaced by the Internet, magazines, newspapers, television and other electronic information sources. Perhaps the best known town crier in all of American history was Paul Revere. However, the tradition precedes his famous ride from Boston to Lexington and carries great significance for us today.

ATTENDANTS AND FRIENDS

In Greek literature, the public crier was the attendant of a prince, but not just an ordinary attendant as we think of the word. Raised above the status of other servants, the crier was given a respect and status similar to a friend.

As believers, we serve the Prince of Peace. Jesus said:

No longer do I call you slaves, for the slave does not know what his master is doing; but I have called you friends, for all things that I have heard from My father I have made known to you.

John 15:15, NASB

Prince Jesus has raised us to a status like that of the town crier. We are His friends, and He says that He will make known to us everything He has heard from the Father.

The Greek word translated as *make known* is the same word used in Ephesians 3:10. What does that mean to us as intercessors? It means that we are not giving just a random outcry, but we are participating in a process released from Heaven.

God the Father makes known (*gnoridzo*) His intentions to Jesus. Jesus makes known (*gnoridzo*) the Father's intentions to the Church. And the Church makes known (*gnoridzo*) the intentions of God to the evil powers through proclamation, or *kerusso*. The result is celestial breakthrough.

DEPUTIES OF THE PRINCE

A town crier was a deputy of the prince and, as such, was given a herald's staff. This scepter in his hands made it clear that, as he carried out his commission, he did so under the prince's authorization.

A *scepter* can be defined as "a rod or wand borne in the hand as an emblem of regal or imperial power." It is also defined as "a royal or imperial power or authority."

God said in His Word:

The scepter will not depart from Judah,

nor the ruler's staff from between his feet,

until he to whom it belongs shall come

and the obedience of the nations shall be his.   Genesis 49:10, NIV

Gilead is Mine, and Manasseh is Mine;

Ephraim also is the helmet of My head;

Judah is My scepter.

Psalm 60:7, NASB

The LORD will stretch forth Your strong scepter from Zion, saying, "Rule in the midst of Your enemies." Psalm 110:2, NASB

When Jesus arose victorious from the grave, He took back the authority Adam had given away in the garden. Jesus then turned and gave the authority He purchased to those who would follow Him, declaring that whatever they bound or loosed on Earth would be bound or loosed in Heaven:

And I will give unto thee the keys of the kingdom of heaven: and whatsoever thou shalt bind on earth shall be bound in heaven:

and whatsoever thou shalt loose on earth shall be loosed in heaven.
                                                        Matthew 16:19

Proclamation carries with it a nature of binding, commanding and settling. Zodhiates says the word *bind* means "to fasten or to tie up with chains or a cord." Prophetic proclamations released through the mouths of intercessors have the ability to tie up the effect of evil powers like an animal tied with chains or cords.

The verb translated here as *loose*, according to Zodhiates, means "to loosen, break up, destroy, dissolve, unloose, melt or put off." When you loose the powers of darkness from a situation, person or city, the enemy is no longer able to do what he intended to do.

PROTECTED HERALDS

The Greeks believed that a herald who came in wartime must not be harmed. If he was touched, the one who touched him would be subject to the wrath of the one who sent the crier and also the wrath of his gods.

The security of the intercessor is his faith in the power of the blood of Jesus. Intercessors are on assignment in a spiritual war. They have been sent by the Captain of the Hosts to do His bidding. A scepter of authority has been given to them, and they are to rule in the Earth. Protection is provided to secure the safety of the spiritual herald. Any opposition will be dealt with by God.

MAKING STRATEGIC DECLARATIONS

THE CHARACTERISTICS OF CRIERS

There are some general characteristics that apply to all public criers, both historic and current:

THEY ARE UNDER AUTHORITY

A crier was always under the authority of someone else. The crier was only the spokesman. In the same way, intercessors should always be under the authority of the Lord. A submissive spirit to Him is vital.

We also need to submit to others:

Submitting yourselves one to another in the fear of God.
                              Ephesians 5:21

No person is above the need for accountability. Each of us has blind spots. We need the help of those who love us enough to tell us the truth.

THEY CONVEY THE MESSAGE OF THE MASTER

The crier was not to deliver his own message or compromise with the one who was receiving it. He simply delivered the message he was sent to speak, nothing more and nothing less.

THEY ANNOUNCE JUDICIAL VERDICTS

What the public crier announced became law by the actual proclamation he made. All truth is parallel. Jesus, the Righteous Judge, hands the verdict to the intercessor, who then delivers a prophetic proclamation to the evil powers. That verdict is enforced through the proclamation spoken by the intercessor.

Jesus said:

What I tell you in darkness, that speak ye in light: and what ye hear in the ear, that preach ye upon the housetops. Matthew 10:27

THEY DECLARE GOD'S FAVOR

Barbara Wentroble, President of Wentroble Christian Ministries, gives this testimony: When the Lord was ready to move their family, they put their house up for sale. Houses were not selling very well where they lived at the time. They prayed and did everything the realtor told them to do, but after eight months on the market, the house had not yet sold.

Barbara said her spiritual daughter was living with them at the time. Knowing the power of proclamation, this daughter started walking the boundaries of the yard every day praying: "In the name of Jesus, I release the favor of God on this house. I command all blinders to come off the eyes of those people needing this house. 'Eyes, see this house.' 'House, you are sold,' in Jesus' name." The result was that within a couple of weeks the house was sold.

The spiritual daughter had uttered a command or a prophetic proclamation. Notice that with this ballistic prayer, a logistical progression was taken:

1. First, the proclamation was made directly to the house.

2. Second, favor was assigned to the house.

3. Third, the perspective buyer (not just any person, but the person needing the house) was addressed.

4. Fourth, warfare was introduced on behalf of the person needing the house.

5. Fifth, an announcement was made to the house of its destiny.

Paul wrote:

But if our gospel be hid, it is hid to them that are lost: in whom the god of this world hath blinded the minds of them which believe not, lest the light of the glorious gospel of Christ, who is the image of God, should shine unto them. 2 Corinthians 4:3-4

This scripture is referencing the Gospel. All truth is parallel. The Gospel is the truth of God. The will of God is that the truth of God will prevail. In this instance, the sale of the house was the will of God. After the god of this world was restrained, the eye gate was commanded to see the house. This logical progression caused the sale of the house.

Again, Paul wrote:

Notwithstanding the Lord stood with me, and strengthened me; that by me the preaching might be fully known, and that all the Gentiles might hear: and I was delivered out of the mouth of the lion. And the Lord shall deliver me from every evil work, and will preserve me unto his heavenly kingdom: to whom be glory for ever and ever. Amen. 2 Timothy 4:17-18

The Lord stood with me, and strengthened me, in order that through me the proclamation might be fully accomplished, and that all the Gentiles might hear; and I was delivered out of the lion's mouth.
2 Timothy 4:17, ASV

When intercessors are given the right word to speak at the right time, there will be great victory and spiritual breakthroughs. There will be deliverance for God's people, for cities and for nations. Therefore God will provide strength to intercessors so that they can do His bidding.

Jesus will make known to you the intentions of His Father. Then, allow Him to strengthen you so that the prophetic proclamation of His Word can go forth from your mouth without compromise and establish His will on the Earth.

DEVELOPING A MANIFESTO

According to Dictionary.com, a *manifesto* is "a public declaration of intentions, opinions, objectives, or motives, as one issued by a government, sovereign, or organization." U.S. politicians often lay out their policies in a manifesto. Their manifesto states their purpose, their aims and promises to their constituents. In their manifesto document, they reveal who they are and what they stand for. They reveal their mission and who will benefit from the changes they propose.

Jesus proclaimed His manifesto in His teachings to His disciples, and in it He revealed who He was:

One of the two which heard John speak, and followed him, was Andrew, Simon Peter's brother. He first findeth his own brother Simon, and saith unto him, We have found the Messias, which is, being interpreted, the Christ.

John 1:40-41

The woman saith unto him, I know that Messias cometh, which is called Christ: when he is come, he will tell us all things.
Jesus saith unto her, I that speak unto thee am he. John 4:25-26

67

Jesus revealed what He stood for:

The thief comes only in order to steal and kill and destroy. I came that they may have and enjoy life, and have it in abundance (to the full, till it overflows).

John 10:10, AMP

Jesus reveled Himself as Life for those who believed on Him:

Jesus saith unto him, I am the way, the truth, and the life: no man cometh unto the Father, but by me.

John 14:6

Jesus revealed His mission:

The Spirit of the Lord is upon me, because he hath anointed me to preach the gospel to the poor.

Luke 4:18

Jesus revealed who would benefit from the changes He brought:

He hath sent me to heal the brokenhearted, to preach deliverance to the captives, and recovering of sight to the blind, to set at liberty them that are bruised.

Luke 4:18

Jesus declared His redemptive mission in life:

To preach the acceptable year of the Lord.   Luke 4:19

So here's what you need to do: Develop a manifesto of what you believe in very strongly. How do you expect to see yourself in the future? Ask the Holy Spirit to give you an image in your mind of how God sees your future. This will strengthen your determination and motivate you to constantly strive for what you believe He has planned for your life.

The writer of Hebrews advised:

Looking unto Jesus the author and finisher of our faith; who for the joy that was set before him endured the cross, despising the shame, and is set down at the right hand of the throne of God.   Hebrews 12:2

"Looking unto Jesus" ... that is, we must set Him continually before us as our example and our encouragement. We must look to Him for direction, for assistance and for acceptance in all of our challenges. We must be unshakable in our belief—without the need for proof or evidence.

As it was with Him, the joy set before us should be the basis of our manifesto document, revealing who we are and what we stand for. It must reveal our mission and who will benefit from the changes we propose.

Spend the necessary time in prayer, seeking guidance from the Holy Spirit to develop your personal manifesto, your personal articles of faith. What do you believe about your accomplishment, your success, your future? Let the enemy know about it.

CHAPTER 4

EMPLOYING IDENTIFICATION REPENTANCE

And I prayed unto the LORD my God, and made my confession, and said, O Lord, the great and dreadful God, keeping the covenant and mercy to them that love him, and to them that keep his commandments; we have sinned, and have committed iniquity, and have done wickedly, and have rebelled, even by departing from thy precepts and from thy judgments. Daniel 9:4-5

Most Christians are familiar with the concept of personal repentance or *metanoia*. We know that each one of us is personally responsible for our own sin, and that we need to acknowledge that sin, repent of it and turn away from it. But in Old Testament times, guilt and repentance were understood on more of a corporate and national level. When an individual sinned, the whole nation was considered guilty.

For instance, Joshua 7:1 tells us that Achan took some items during the conquest of Jericho that were destined for destruction and hid them for himself. But look what the Scriptures have to say about it:

But the children of Israel committed a trespass in the accursed thing: for

73

Achan, the son of Carmi, the son of Zabdi, the son of Zerah, of the tribe of Judah, took of the accursed thing: and the anger of the LORD was kindled against the children of Israel.   Joshua 7:1

The guilt for what Achan had done was nation wide. In the eleventh verse, God emphasized that Israel had sinned, that the whole nation was guilty, and therefore all were worthy of His judgement:

And the LORD said unto Joshua, Get thee up; wherefore liest thou thus upon thy face? ISRAEL HATH SINNED, and THEY HAVE ALSO TRANSGRESSED my covenant which I commanded them: for they

have even taken of the accursed thing, and have also stolen, and dissembled also, and they have put it even among their own stuff.
Joshua 7:10-11, Emphasis added

The whole nation was under judgement until the sin of that one individual could be dealt with. This shows us that any sin committed by any individual in that nation affected every other individual in the nation. All shared the responsibility, even if they had not personally committed the sin themselves.

There were times when God called the whole nation of Israel together to deal with sin on a corporate level. He called young and old alike to a time of prayer, fasting and confession of sin:

Now in the twenty and fourth day of this month the children of Israel were assembled with fasting, and with sackclothes, and earth upon them. And the seed of Israel separated themselves from all strangers, and stood and confessed their sins, and the iniquities of their fathers.

Nehemiah 9:1-2

At other times, some individual representing the people intervened or mediated between them and God, confessing the sins of the whole nation and pleading for God's righteous judgement on all the people to be turned away:

And I [Daniel] prayed unto the LORD *my God, and made my*

confession, and said, O Lord, the great and dreadful God, keeping the covenant and mercy to them that love him, and to them that keep his commandments; We have sinned, and have committed iniquity, and have done wickedly, and have rebelled, even by departing from thy precepts and from thy judgments: neither have we hearkened unto thy servants the prophets, which spake in thy name to our kings, our princes, and our fathers, and to all the people of the land.

O Lord, to us belongeth confusion of face, to our kings, to our princes, and to our fathers, because we have sinned against thee. To the Lord our God belong mercies and forgivenesses, though we have rebelled against him; neither have we obeyed the voice of the LORD our God, to walk in his laws, which he set before us by his servants the prophets. Yea, all Israel have transgressed thy law, even by departing, that they might not obey thy voice; therefore the curse is poured upon us, and the oath that is written in the law of Moses the servant of God, because we have sinned against him.

O Lord, according to all thy righteousness, I beseech thee, let thine anger and thy fury be turned away from thy city Jerusalem, thy holy mountain: because for our sins, and for the iniquities of our fathers, Jerusalem and thy people are become a reproach to all that are about us. Now therefore, O our

God, hear the prayer of thy servant, and his supplications, and cause thy face to shine upon thy sanctuary that is desolate, for the Lord's sake. O my God, incline thine ear, and hear; open thine eyes, and behold our desolations, and the city which is called by thy name: for we do not present our supplications before thee for our righteousnesses, but for thy great mercies. O Lord, hear; O Lord, forgive; O Lord, hearken and do; defer not, for thine own sake, O my God: for thy city and thy people are called by thy name.

Daniel 9:4-6, 8-11 and 16-19

Moses was one of those who mediated between God and the rest of the people of Israel. He was the leader of a large disgruntled crowd of ex-slaves, and they were rebellious, complaining, difficult, and irritating to deal with. At times, they tested Moses' patience to the limit. They also tested God's patience to the limit, and provoked His severest judgement.

After Moses had been given the Ten Commandments and while he was still on Mt. Sinai communicating with God, the people turned away from Him and made a golden calf and worshipped it. Because of this gross rebellion, God proposed to consume them all:

And the LORD said unto Moses, I have seen this people, and, behold, it is a stiffnecked people: now therefore let me alone, that my wrath may wax hot against them, and that I may consume them: and I will make of thee a great nation.

Exodus 32:9-10

Thankfully Moses' intercession saved them. Even though he was himself disgusted at what the people had done, he stood with them, identifying himself with them and seeking to make atonement for their sin:

He prayed, "Alas, this people have sinned a great sin; they have made for themselves gods of gold. But now, if thou wilt forgive their sin - and if not, blot me, I pray thee, out of thy book which thou hast written."

Exodus 32:31-32, ASV

In effect, Moses was saying to God, "If You intend to destroy these people, You will have to destroy me too, because I am one of them." Amazingly, through Moses' identification with his people, and his supplication for forgiveness on their behalf, God changed His decision and forgave them everything.

Throughout his lifetime Moses continued to be the primary mediator between the people of Israel and God. He interceded, in times of crisis and rebellion, for the whole of Israel. And many opportunities presented themselves for him to stand on their behalf.

When they had worshipped the golden calf was just one such opportunity. Then, to deal with the sins that the people of Israel committed every day,

God set up another system of mediation, that of the priesthood.

The priesthood consisted of the priests. These were initially Aaron as High Priest and his sons as priests. Later they were his descendants. Part of the work of the priesthood was representing the people before God, confessing their sins and seeking forgiveness on their behalf. Usually this was done by the High Priest himself.

DANIEL'S PRAYER OF IDENTIFICATION REPENTANCE

Daniel was a man who walked in God's ways from his youth. As a young man, it was said that he was:

Without any physical defect, handsome, showing aptitude for every kind of learning, well informed, quick to understand and qualified to serve in the king's palace.

Daniel 1:4, NIV

It would benefit us to see more of that passage:

And the king spake unto Ashpenaz the master of his eunuchs, that he should bring certain of the children of Israel, and of the king's seed, and of the princes; children in whom was no blemish, but well favoured, and skillful in all wisdom, and cunning in knowledge, and under-standing science, and such as had ability in them to stand in the king's palace, and whom they might teach the learning and the tongue of the Chaldeans.   Daniel 1:3-4

Daniel demonstrated his heart for God early by choosing to take a stand for Him and not defile himself by eating unclean foods (food sacrificed to idols) from the king's table, This was very bold because he had only recently been taken captive to Babylon. But God blessed Daniel for his stand for holiness, and prospered him in every way:

> *Then the king made Daniel a great man, and gave him many great gifts, and made him ruler over the whole province of Babylon and chief of the governors over all the wise men of Babylon.* Daniel 2:48

Later, after King Darius made it illegal to pray, Daniel risked his life to remain faithful to God and continue his discipline of prayer. Daniel was clearly a righteous man who honored God from his youth, and as a result, God honored him.

Still, in Daniel 9, we find this righteous man praying a prayer of confession, repenting for the sins of all Israel. He did not say, "Our fathers committed this sin," "our ancestors did that," or even "they sinned against You." Instead, we see him taking upon himself the position of the people he was praying for. He said:

And I prayed unto the LORD my God, and made my confession, and said, O Lord, the great and dreadful God, keeping the covenant and mercy to them that love him, and to

them that keep his commandments;
we have sinned, and have committed
iniquity, and have done wickedly,
and have rebelled, even by depart-
ing from thy precepts and from thy
judgments.　　　　　Daniel 9:4-5

Daniel was saying:

- **We** have sinned and done wrong.
- **We** have been wicked.
- **We** have rebelled.
- **We** have turned away from Your commands and laws.

And the prayer goes on. Over and over, we see Daniel using the words *we* and *our* when referring to those who had sinned. He took ownership of sins that were committed before he was even born, so we know that he did not personally commit these sins. However, as an intercessor, he stepped into the place of being identified with those who did sin.

Daniel then offered his sincere repentance before God for the sins that were committed and asked God to release grace and forgiveness to all the people:

Now therefore, O our God, hear the prayer of thy servant, and his supplications, and cause thy face to shine upon thy sanctuary that is desolate, for the Lord's sake. O my God, incline thine ear, and hear; open thine eyes, and behold our desolations, and the city which is called by thy name: for we do not present our supplications before thee for our righteousnesses, but for thy great mercies. O Lord, hear; O Lord, forgive; O Lord, hearken and do; defer not, for thine own sake, O my God: for thy city and thy people are called by thy name.

Daniel 9:17-19

Daniel, then, is a perfect example of what identification repentance is all about. If there was ever a person who did not conform to what the nation did, it was Daniel. And yet the Lord lead him to identify with the sins of his fore-fathers and sincerely repent for them.

The Bible makes it clear that, on the basis of Daniel's personal relationship with God, his prayers were heard and answered:

And whiles I was speaking, and praying, and confessing my sin and the sin of my people Israel, and presenting my supplication before the LORD my God for the holy mountain of my God; yea, whiles I was speaking in prayer, even the man Gabriel, whom I had seen in the vision at the beginning, being caused to fly swiftly, touched me about the time of the evening oblation. And he informed me, and talked with me, and said, O Daniel, I am now come forth to give thee skill and understanding. At the beginning of thy supplications the commandment came forth, and I am come to shew thee; for thou art greatly beloved: therefore understand the matter, and consider the vision. Daniel 9:20-23

Many Bible scholars believe that it was Daniel's identification repentance, under the Holy Spirit's prompting, that paved the way for the city of Jerusalem and the great Temple to be rebuilt.

The answer to Daniels' prayer was given immediately, but he had to war and persist in the Spirit to see it through. If God calls you to employ identification repentance, stand firm and confident in the knowledge that He will hear your prayers and answer them, just as He did with Daniel.

CHAPTER 5

KNOWING WHERE TERRITORIAL SPIRITS OPERATE

But the LORD is the true God, He is the living God, and an everlasting king. ... Thus shall ye say unto them, The gods that have not made the heavens, and the earth, even they shall perish from the earth, and from under these heavens.

Jeremiah 10:10-11

One of the major differences that separate Christian beliefs from those of the pagans is our understanding and worship of one God. A religion of monotheism worships one God, versus the worship and the recognition of many gods. *Monolatrism* or *monolatry* in Greek is defined as "the recognition of the existence of many gods, but with the consistent worship of only one deity." [3]

There are and have been many gods, and many of them were recognized as deities that operated over cities or regions. For example:

And the servants of the king of Syria said unto him, Their gods are gods of the hills; therefore they

3. Frank E. Eakin, Jr., *The Religion and Culture of Israel* (Boston: Allyn and Bacon, 1971), p70

were stronger than we, but let us fight against them in the plain, and surely we shall be stronger than they. 1 Kings 20:23

But the prince of the kingdom of Persia withstood me one and twenty days; but, lo Michael, one of the chief princes, came to help me, and I remained there with the kings of Persia. Daniel 10:13

We see gods and goddesses who were over people groupings:

Because that they have forsaken me, and have worshiped Ashtoreth the goddess of the Zidonians, Chemosh, the god of the Moabites, and Milcom, the god of the children of Ammon, and have not walked in my ways, to do that which is right in mine eyes, and to keep my statutes and my judgments, as did David his father ...　　1 Kings 11:33

We also see gods who were associated with physical things:

The children gather wood, and the fathers kindle the fire, and the women knead their dough, to make cakes to the queen of heaven, and to pour out drink offerings unto other gods, that they may provoke me to anger.　　Jeremiah 7:18

Then he brought me to the door of the gate of the LORD's house which was toward the north, and,

behold, there sat women weeping
for Tammuz.   Ezekiel 8:14

The ancient Egyptians had many such gods. When God sent Moses to call down plagues on that land, it is interesting to note that each plague demonstrated the power of the one true God and the impotency of the gods of Egypt.

The first sign the Lord had given Moses was that his rod turned into a serpent and then back into a rod. Later, in Egypt this happened again. When Pharaoh's magicians tried to duplicate this sign, Moses' serpent consumed the serpents from the rods of the magicians:

And the LORD *spake unto Moses*
and unto Aaron, saying, When

Pharaoh shall speak unto you, saying, Shew a miracle for you: then thou shalt say unto Aaron, Take thy rod, and cast it before Pharaoh, and it shall become a serpent.

Exodus 7:8-9

To the Egyptians, the serpent was a symbol of royal authority. A serpent even formed part of the Pharaoh's crown.

Hapi was the Egyptian god of the Nile, and he proved powerless, as God turned all the water of Egypt into blood:

Thus saith the LORD, In this thou shalt know that I am the LORD: behold, I will smite with the rod that is in mine hand upon the waters which are in the river, and they shall be turned to blood.

Exodus 7:17

Heka, an Egyptian goddess, had a frogs head, so it was in mockery of her that God used Moses to bring forth an abundance of frogs upon the land:

And if thou refuse to let them go, behold, I will smite all thy borders with frogs. Exodus 8:2

Shu, the Egyptian god of the air, was not able to stand against the plague of flies God sent through Moses:

Else, if thou wilt not let my people go, behold, I will send swarms of flies upon thee, and upon thy servants, and upon thy people, and into thy houses: and the houses of the Egyptians shall be full of swarms of flies, and also the ground whereon they are.

Exodus 8:21

The plague God sent against the cattle was a direct assault on the Egyptian practice of worshipping cows:

Behold, the hand of the LORD is upon thy cattle which is in the field, upon the horses, upon the asses, upon the camels, upon the oxen, and upon the sheep: there shall be a very grievous murrain.

Exodus 9:3

When Moses and Aaron threw ashes into the air, and a plague of boils resulted, this was a blatantly mockery of the Egyptian gods Sutech and Typhon, whose usual offering was the ashes of sacrificial victims:

And the LORD *said unto Moses and unto Aaron, Take to you handfuls of ashes of the furnace, and let Moses sprinkle it toward the heaven in the sight of Pharaoh. And it shall become small dust in all the land of Egypt, and shall be a boil breaking forth with blains upon man, and upon beast, throughout all the land of Egypt. And they took ashes of the furnace, and stood before Pharaoh; and Moses sprinkled it up toward heaven; and it became a boil breaking forth with blains upon man, and upon beast.*

Exodus 9:8-10

As hail fell from the sky, none of the Egyptian gods (considered to be from Heaven) could stop it:

Behold, tomorrow about this time I will cause it to rain a very grievous hail, such as hath not been in Egypt since the foundation thereof even until now.

Exodus 9:18

Part of Egypt's beauty came from the many sycamore trees that grew there. But when God sent the locusts, those beautiful trees were all devoured:

And Moses and Aaron came in unto Pharaoh, and said unto him, Thus saith the LORD God of the Hebrews, How long wilt thou refuse to humble thyself before me? Let my people go, that they may serve me. Else, if thou refuse to let my people go, behold, tomorrow will I bring the locusts into thy coast: and they shall cover the face of the earth, that one cannot be able to see the earth: and they shall eat the residue of that which is escaped, which remaineth unto you from the hail, and shall eat every tree which groweth for you out of the field. Exodus 10:3-5

The plague of darkness that God sent showed the impotency of Ra, the sun god:

And the LORD said unto Moses, Stretch out thine hand toward heaven, that there may be darkness over the land of Egypt, even darkness which may be felt. And Moses stretched forth his hand toward heaven; and there was a thick darkness in all the land of Egypt three days. Exodus 10:21-22

When God was about to bring the final judgement upon Egypt, Moses made a direct declaration. The Lord was about to destroy all of the firstborn in the land:

For I will pass through the land of Egypt on this night, and will smite all the firstborn in the land of Egypt, both man and beast; and against all the gods of Egypt I will execute judgment; I am the LORD.

Exodus 12:12

Every time God had Moses speak to Pharaoh, He had him say, "Let My people go, that they may serve Me and worship Me." Always remember: the bottom line is for the people of God to be freed in order that they might be able to serve and worship Him.

These scriptures make it clear that certain deities or evil spirits work over regions or people groups, but God uses His people to come against such deities:

Thou art my battle axe and weapons of war; for with thee will I break in pieces the nations, and with thee will I destroy kingdoms; and with thee will I break in pieces the horse and his rider, and with thee will I break in pieces the chariot and his rider. Jeremiah 51:20-21

For we wrestle not against flesh and blood, but against principalities, against powers, against the rulers of the darkness of this world, against wickedness in high places.

Ephesians 6:12

Submit yourselves therefore to God. Resist the devil, and he will flee from you. James 4:7

In the time of the judges, God gave clear instructions to Gideon to bring down the stronghold of Baal, his father's god, and to establish the area for the Lord. The King James Version of the Bible uses the term *"altar of Baal,"* which simply meant the place from which that deity was operating:

> *Then Gideon built an altar there unto the Lord, and called it Jehovah Shalom; unto this day it is yet in Ophrah of the Abiezrites.*
>
> *And it came to pass the same night, that the Lord said unto him, Take thy father's young bullock, even the second bullock of seven years old, and throw down the altar of Baal that they father hath, and cut down the grove that is by it; and build an altar unto the Lord thy God upon the top of this rock in the ordered place, and take the second bullock,*

and offer a burn sacrifice with the wood of the grove which thou shalt cut down.   Judges 6:24-26

Gideon was so in awe of God and so grateful for His wonder-working power that he built an altar to the Him. However, as pleased as the Lord was with Gideon's devotion, He asked more of him. He also wanted the altar of the other god brought down.

Today, God does not intend for us to serve and worship Him while living comfortably in the midst of other gods. He is a jealous God and wants us actively working against that which is an abomination to His holiness and truth. [4]

If you and I are to successfully deal with and overcome false gods, we must

───────────

4. Adapted from http://ausprayernet.org.au/teaching/

know and understand how they work and then be willing to take a stand against them and bring them down once and for all.

CHAPTER 6

APPLYING THE BLOOD OF CHRIST ON BEHALF OF CITIES

And the blood shall be to you for a token upon the houses where ye are; and when I see the blood, I will pass over you, and the plague shall not be upon you to destroy you, when I smite the land of Egypt.

Exodus 12:13

In the book of Exodus we see the Lord declaring to Moses that whatever house on which they put the blood of a lamb, its inhabitants would be spared from the work of the plague. In this verse the King James Version uses the word *token* instead of sign. *Strong's* defines *token* as "a signal, flag, beacon, evidence or mark." The Lord said that the blood would be a *token* for them. In other words, as they applied the blood, it was to be evidence for them of His promise. As they heard the cries in the streets, they could only be reminded that God was faithful to keep His promises to His people.

We are children of the promise. Therefore God is still delivering us.

Now we, brethren, as Isaac was, are the children of promise.

Galatians 4:28

In the same verse, the word *see* means "to consider, approve or advise self." Just think, when the Lord saw the blood on the door, He advised Himself to spare the Israelites by passing over them.

We are clearly taught in the Scriptures that the blood of Christ far surpasses the work of the blood of lambs and goats. If the Lord paid such attention to the blood of an earthly lamb, how much more is He honoring the presence of the blood of His only begotten Son.

In the book of Leviticus chapter 14, we read of the instructions given to the priests for the cleansing of lepers. Leprosy was not only a severe disease, but in the Scriptures also represented sin. The Levitical account shows the sprinkling of blood being used to bring about their cleansing. As we sprinkle, or apply, the blood of Jesus in prayer, His authentic blood does an even greater work than the blood of goats, bullocks, and rams.

We also read a prophetic word concerning the work of the blood of Jesus in the book of Isaiah:

So shall he sprinkle many nations; the kings shall shut their mouths at him: for that which had not been told them shall they see; and that which they had not heard shall they consider. Isaiah 52:15

So shall he startle many nations;
    kings shall shut their mouths because of him;

*for that which has not been told
them they shall see,*

> *and that which they have not
heard they shall understand.*

Isaiah 52:14, RSV

This word *startle* in Hebrew is translated as *sprinkle*. Just as if you were to take water with your fingers and flick it in someone's face, they would be startled, and you would have their attention. That is what Christ did with His blood. He got the attention of nations and kings, and the blood caused them to see and hear that which they had not previously seen or heard.

As we stand in the gap for our cities and apply the blood of Jesus, we get their attention. We have legislative authority to apply the blood, releasing it so that it can do what it was designed to do.

The following scriptures tell us of the work of the blood of Christ.

That at time ye were without Christ, being aliens from the commonwealth of Israel, and strangers from the covenants of promise, having no hope, and without God in the world: but now in Christ Jesus ye who sometimes were far off are made nigh by the BLOOD of Christ.
Ephesians 2:12-13, Emphasis added

And, having made peace through the BLOOD of his cross, by him to reconcile all things unto himself, by him I say, whether they be things in earth or things in heaven.

Colossians 1:20, Emphasis added

How much more shall the BLOOD of Christ, who through the eternal Spirit offered himself without spot to God, purge your conscience from dead works to serve the living God?

Hebrews 9:14, Emphasis added

For as much as ye know that ye were not redeemed with corruptible things, as silver and gold, from your vain conversation received by tradition from your fathers; but with the precious BLOOD of Christ, as of a lamb without blemish and without spot.

1 Peter 1:18-19, Emphasis added

As we apply the blood of Jesus over the souls in our cities, we are covering them with that which will draw them near to God, cleansing their conscience to give them an ease to serve the living God. We are loosing the blood of Jesus to sanctify, redeem and reconcile:

And to Jesus the mediator of the new covenant, and to the BLOOD of sprinkling, that speaketh better things than that of Abel.

Hebrews 12:24, Emphasis added

The word *speaketh,* used in the King James Version, means "to speak, talk, tell, or to utter words." This phrase *better things* means "stronger, nobler, and better."

The blood of Jesus preaches, tells or utters the dominion, the power and the nobility of Christ. As I apply the blood over souls, that blood speaks to them and over them.

As God's people, we are truth-carriers. We hold the strategic weapons to bring down strongholds. As we work diligently to enforce the will of God in the Earth realm, we are to apply the blood of Jesus in our daily activities so as to make an impression on unacceptable situations. By "unacceptable," I mean situations that do not line up with God's intended purpose.

We must diligently do what the Word has taught us for the enforcement of Kingdom principles. We *"can do all things through Christ"*:

> *I can do all things through Christ which strengtheneth me.*
>
> Philippians 4:13

This includes praying and warring on behalf of our family and our cities. The Berean Literal Bible translates this verse as, *"I have strength for all things in the One strengthening me."* Amen and Amen!

CHAPTER 7

CLAIMING GOD'S WISDOM

This wisdom descendeth not from above, but is earthly, sensual, devilish.   James 3:15

Strong's says that *wisdom* is "to be wise in earthly or spiritually and to be skillful or to have good sense." *Webster's Dictionary* defines *wisdom* as "the quality of being wise, the faculty of making the best use of knowledge, experience, understanding, etc., good judgment, sagacity, penetrating intelligence, quickness or acuteness of discernment." Those who are not in Christ are under the influence of earthly wisdom. Those who have Christ have the advantage of having both earthly and spiritual wisdom.

Earthly wisdom is deceitful and oppressive. It affects the way people think in every arena of life. God's Word gives us a clear description of this wisdom.

This wisdom descendeth not from above, but is earthly [worldly], *sensual* [soulish], *and devilish* [demon-like]. James 3:15

As we pray on behalf of our cities or neighborhoods, we need to bind up earthly wisdom and loose God's wisdom. When we do this, we provide an environment for souls to get out from under the unrighteous counsel of the world, the soul, and demons. This will help them be able to hear the message the Spirit of Wisdom is preaching.

Does this great wisdom have a message that she preaches? In studying the following passage from Proverbs, we can see that she does.

Wisdom crieth without; she uttereth her voice in the streets: she crieth in the chief place of concourse, in the openings of the gates: in the city she uttereth her words, saying, How long, ye simple ones, will ye love simplicity? and the scorners delight in their scorning, and fools hate knowledge? Turn you at my reproof: behold, I will pour out my spirit unto you, I will make known my words unto you.

Proverbs 1:20-23

Wisdom crieth [through the idea of accosting a person, to call a person by name, preach, publish], *without: she uttereth* [with a great deal of latitude, bestow, grant, distribute appoint, command, require] *her voice in the streets; she crieth in the chief place of concourse* [any place that is in great commotion or tumult, where there is rage, war, clamor], *in the openings of the gates; in the city she uttereth her words, saying, How long, ye simple* [silly, seducible, foolish] *ones will ye love simplicity? and the scorners delight in*

122

their scorning, and fools [stupid, silly, foolish] *hate knowledge? Turn you* [turn back, repent, be restored, convert], *at my reproof* [chastisement, correction, and contradiction, proof]: *behold, I will pour out my spirit unto you, I will make known my words unto you.*

We can see from this scripture that wisdom preaches to all people the same message: repent and be restored to God. She goes boldly and aggressively, with the idea of accosting a person, and to all places—open places, the streets, where there's riots, gates and where there are souls. She speaks to many classes of people—simple ones, fools, scorners and, of course, the saints.

In the book of James we see evidence of God's mercy, as we read that He gives wisdom to all men and that He doesn't rebuke them as He gives out these gifts:

If any of you lack wisdom, let him ask of God, that giveth to all men liberally, and upbraideth not; and it shall be given him.   James 1:5

But the wisdom that is from above is first pure, then peaceable, gentle, and easy to be intreated, full of mercy and good fruits, without partiality, and without hypocrisy.
                                        James 3:17

When we claim God's wisdom, we can operate from a stance of power.

His wisdom is informing. In the realm of His wisdom, we can make objective and informed decisions to engage the enemy and when and how to do it.

CHAPTER 8

USING PERSONAL PRAYER MAPPING

Son of man, I have made thee a watchman unto the house of Israel: therefore hear the word at my mouth, and give them warning from me. Ezekiel 3:17

I have set watchmen upon thy walls, O Jerusalem, which shall never hold their peace day nor night: ye that make mention of the LORD, keep not silence. Isaiah 62:6

But if the watchman see the sword come, and blow not the trumpet, and the people be not warned; if the sword come, and take any person from among them, he is taken away in his iniquity; but his blood will I require at the watchman's hand.

Ezekiel 33:6

Personal prayer mapping is the name given to a process that involves finding and identifying the origins of the things that require prayer. We must understand the issues of our own soul and the souls of those we love and are praying for.

The events of our past affect the way we feel, behave, and interact in the present. If we want to change our current behavior and emotions, we need to change the way the past has affected us. [5] The key is to uniquely target those areas in prayer and move away from anemic prayers, such as: "Please change my husband and make him quit drinking." Through prayer mapping, you can trace the roots of the soul and understand why people engage in certain behaviors. With this information you can pray more strategically.

If your prayer is simple (the first dimension), by moving to more concise request (the second dimension), you could pray about the things in his heart that encourage him to drink excessively. In this dimension, you pray that God would remove the influences in his life that enable him to abuse the alcohol.

5. Praying Medic, *Emotional Healing in 3 Easy Steps* (Gilbert, AZ: Inkity Press, 2015)

Instead of praying something like: "Please be with Aunt Mary who is having surgery, and let her know You love her," you could pray from a second dimension more broadly, such as:

- "God, please help the surgeon to rest well tonight."
- "God, send Your angels to fill Aunt Mary's room with light and glory."
- "God, let the surgeon's hands become as Your hands."

You can see that if you start thinking this way, you can easily come up with a customized prayer for yours or someone else's needs.

To truly understand and practice personal prayer mapping, we need an understanding of our enemy, because we need to see his patterns. We need to have eyes to see how he deceives, tempts, and devours. We need to recognize what a stronghold is. Once we learn these things, we will very quickly begin to see his fingerprints on families in the way they struggle. Then, we are able to personalize our prayer approach.

WHAT EXACTLY IS PERSONALIZED PRAYER MAPPING

Prayer mapping is patterned from a concept associated with land masses. Instead of relating to land masses, we specialize on the individual person and the inner life of an individual.

Personalized prayer mapping is very much like praying through a genogram.

A genogram (pronounced: jen-uh-gram) is a graphic representation of a family tree that displays detailed data on relationships among individuals. It goes beyond a traditional family tree by allowing the user to analyze hereditary patterns and psychological factors that disrupt relationships.

Genograms allow a therapist and his patient to quickly identify and understand various patterns in the patient's family history which may have had an influence on the patient's current state of mind. The genogram maps out relationships and traits that may otherwise be missed on a pedigree chart.

Genogram, as defined by Dictionary. com, is "a graphic representation of the personalities and interplay of generations within a family, used to identify repetitive patterns of behavior; a psychological family tree." *Merriam-Webster* defines *genogram* as "a diagram outlining the history of the behavior patterns (as of divorce, abortion, or suicide) of a family's members over several generations in order to recognize and understand past influences on current behavior patterns; also a similar diagram detailing the medical history of the members of a family as a means of assessing a family member's risk of developing disease."

Prayer mapping uses the same technique that is used in mapping social and physical features. Because all truth is parallel, it is just as effective in spiritual instances.

Prayer mapping then becomes a graphic representation of spiritual conditions and cause of death of family members going back several generations, and is used especially to assess spiritual disease risk. It puts emphases on looking inside the individual and others from a spiritual vantage point.

Scriptural principles become our network, and the Holy Spirit is our Counselor and Guide, enabling us to diagnose our own spiritual diseases. We identify those elements that are impeding our spiritual growth and freedom and then work with those individual fragments in prayer. In counseling or in listening prayer, an issue is isolated and then dealt with.

In prayer mapping, many issues are targeted at once, and the results are dynamic. Many times, a well-constructed prayer map can do, in just six months, what would take a counseling process years.

Simply put, a personalized prayer map consists of pieces of information about the inner life of the soul, clues that can then be redirected to a spiritual strategy and to make our prayer more direct and intentional.

This process is entirely dependent upon our yieldedness to the Holy Spirit. It is the supernatural wisdom He imparts that will produce a series of prayer strategies that are Spirit-led and, therefore, effective. Try it!

CHAPTER 9

NAVIGATING THE SPIRITUAL REALM

In your anger do not sin: Do not let the sun go down while you are still angry, and do not give the devil a foothold. Ephesians 4:27, NIV

To understand prayer mapping better, pull out a map of your state and look at it. What does it tell you? It shows roads, highways, directions, points of interest, topical information such as mountains and waterways, elevations, city and town names, distance information, locations of parks and probably some blowups of major cities and their road systems. The map makes it easy to navigate around the state. Think what it would be like trying to visit a city within your state by taking off in a car without a map in the hope you would eventually hit upon the right spot.

A prayer map, or spiritual map, tries to provide information in the spiritual realm as a regular map does in the natural realm. It is looking at a geographic territory from a spiritual perspective.

The Greek word *topos* gives us a clear indication that Satan use his weapons in spiritual geographic territories. The Scriptures verify that there are locations in the spirit where war activity against you operate.

Paul wrote to the Ephesians:

Neither give place to the devil.
Ephesians 4:27

This word *place* is translated from *topos* in the Greek. According to *Strong's,* it denotes "a place, a region, a seat or an opportunity." According to the *NAS Exhaustive Concordance,* this word denotes "areas, such as locality, occasion, opportunity, passenger, regions, or room."

A close observation of the original intent of the word *place* implies that Satan takes every occasion and opportunity to intercept the plan of God for your life. If you allow him to do it, he will become your passenger as you navigate through life. He will sit in the passenger seat and quietly suggest an alternate path.

Preparing a prayer map for yourself, or another individual, a city, a town, or a region positions you in the power realm of the second dimension. In that power realm, you pray more effectively to bring that territory under the Lordship of Jesus Christ.

A prayer map assesses the current and historical spiritual conditions that may present open doors for a foothold for the enemy.

Paul continued:

"In your anger do not sin:" Do not let the sun go down while you

are still angry, and do not give the devil a foothold.

Ephesians 4:26-27, NIV

With prayer mapping, information is revealed in identifiable areas so that a strategy may be drawn to recover any ground currently in the possession of Satan and his demonic cohorts.

DEVELOPING A PERSONAL PRAYER MAP [6]

WHAT GOES INTO A PRAYER MAP?

A prayer map consists of all the scraps of information that can be gathered about a person, a person's family, or a region that will give clues to what is really going on behind the scenes spiritually. When I am moving in this

---

6. See the appendix for a personal prayer map template.

vein, I ask God for a detective's anointing so that I can prayer map in the Spirit. I then gather clues, piece them together, apply some natural and supernatural wisdom, pray for help from the Holy Spirit and, in this way, come up with a prayer map that can be the basis of effective prayer.

Look specifically for blessings and curses that influence the person, the person's family, or the territory of interest.

HOW TO MAKE A GENOGRAM

As noted in a previous chapter, a genogram is a family map or history that uses special symbols to describe relationships, major events, and the dynamics of a family over multiple generations. Think of it as an extremely detailed family tree. For a spiritual genogram, we are only concerned with anything that translates into spiritual behavior.

As noted, mental health and medical professionals often use genograms to identify patterns of mental and physical illnesses, such as depression, bipolar disorder, cancer and other genetic diseases. According to Wikihow, the methods you may use to develop a genogram are as follows:

1. Develop a set of questions to ask yourself and your relatives that may reflect behaviors that could lead to negative results. Beginning with your grandmother, did she or any family member abuse drugs or alcohol? Did she or any family member have any

mental or physical illnesses? If so, what were/are they?

2. Write down what you know already. Chances are, you already know quite a bit about your family history.

3. Look at your own history. You have a wealth of information within your own personal history that can help you with a baseline.

4. Learn family relationships. You need to know how everyone in your family is connected. Research the unions between family members, gathering information on marriages, divorces, children, etc. Take note of who is married, who is divorced, who may be living together outside of marriage. Is anyone widowed or separated?

5. Learn the emotional relationships your family members have had. Uncovering the answers to the emotional questions will be useful when trying to determine any psychological factors in your family. Do members get along with each other? Look for patterns of abuse or neglect. You can go even further and differentiate between physical and emotional issues.

6. Look carefully to see what patterns can be identified. There may be hereditary patterns or particular psychological tendencies that are very noticeable when grouped together in this way.

Be attentive to the leading of the Holy Spirit to expose every possible open door that may have been the causation for the attack of the enemy.

For more information on how to make and use a genogram, you may want to visit the following sites:

- http://www.aafp.org/fpm/2001/0300/fpm20010300p49-rt1.pdf
- http://dhhs.ne.gov/children_family_services/Documents/a1FGenSym.pdf
- http://en.wikipedia.org/wiki/Genogram
- http://www.genograms.org/create.html
- http://dhhs.ne.gov/children_family_services/Documents/

a1FGenSym.pdf

- http://www.aafp.org/fpm/2001/0300/fpm20010300p49-rt1.pdf
- http://www.genopro.com/genogram/templates/

CHAPTER 10

UNDERSTANDING LEVELS OF BALLISTIC PRAYER

Praying always with all prayer and supplication in the Spirit, and watching thereunto with all perseverance and supplication for all saints. Ephesians 6:18

There are different levels of *Ballistic Apostolic Prayer*:

Personal Level Warfare: This relates to our personal warfare. It could be sickness, a problem with sex or other sins such as greed or pride. Examples of this level are:

- When families in a region are likely to have at least one drug addict among them
- When a father and mother think they still have their God-given authority over their married children
- When a father and mother abuse their children

Corporate Level Warfare: In the corporate level of warfare, there are leaders, rulers, and people in authority. Emphasis is on school principals and teachers, pastors of a church, other organizational or ministry leaders, and other leaders, rulers or authorities. Some examples of this level are:

- A school principal and/or teacher abusing their students in school
- Greed spreading in a church or in a denomination

Regional Level Warfare: This has the greatest influence, for it touches a whole region and many generations. This goes beyond churches, beyond organizations, and beyond local communities. Some examples of this level are:

- When an entire region is filled with cheating and greed
- When laws are adopted that attempt to change the culture of generations.

In this level of warfare, you advance the Kingdom of God and wage a war for the whole region or country. When you advance and wage war for a whole region, the effectiveness of your warfare will increase. God will usually use His apostles and apostolic teams to advance His Kingdom in this level of warfare.

Even in the darkest places of this Earth (including the Communist countries) where God has sent His anointed servants, the Kingdom of God is advancing. Will you do your part?

CHAPTER 11

CHANGING THE ATMOSPHERE

*For I know the thoughts that I think toward you, saith the L*ORD*, thoughts of peace, and not of evil, to give you an expected end.*

Jeremiah 29:11

Merriam-Webster defines *atmosphere* as "the air of a locality, a surrounding influence or an environment." The atmosphere is "the pervading tone or mood of a place." What is true of localities is also true of our families, our ministries and our workplaces, or any group, church or sub-community. It is also true of our individual lives.

Have you stopped to consider what the prevailing atmosphere of your life, family, church, ministry or locality is right now? Many things can impact the atmosphere of a region.

Look at your history. Any injustices that you have suffered may have affected your situation today. The distinctive culture of your neighborhood, or memories and emotions concerning events that have occurred locally may have had a tremendous effect.

Another cause may be spiritual strongholds that are unique to your area. Judgments and opinions related to politics, people, systems and organizations may also play a significant part in your way of life.

There are factors from the past and also things taking place right now that may be affecting the atmosphere of your family or your personal life. The amazing thing is that in spite of all these things, an atmosphere can be changed. This is the power of the Gospel. Didn't God say:

For I know the thoughts that I think toward you, saith the LORD, thoughts of peace, and not of evil, to give you an expected end.

Jeremiah 29:11

In the book of Acts, we learn of a great revival that took place in the city of Samaria. That city had once been bound in deception to sorcery, but when the people heard the Good News about Jesus, the atmosphere of the entire city became one of great joy:

And there was great joy in that city.
Acts 8:8

As believers, we do not have to put up with or be affected by a negative atmosphere. We can partner with God to influence and transform the atmosphere around us.

In Genesis 1, we read of how the Earth's atmosphere was dark and empty. When God spoke a let-there-be word, that atmosphere was transformed. Light came, and life came. When we speak in agreement with what our heavenly Father is speaking, creative power is released for the fulfillment of His plans.

We must also release a let-there-be word from the God of the universe, for no word from Him will ever fail:

For no word from God shall be void of power. Luke 1:37, ASV

But how do we actually change the atmosphere? It begins with words:

Death and life are in the power of the tongue: and they that love it shall eat the fruit thereof.
Proverbs 18:21

The Bible tells us that life-giving power is released when God's people speak words of life. Following are five ways that you can speak prophetic, life-giving words that will transform the atmosphere around you.

1. FOCUS ON AND TALK ABOUT WHAT GOD IS DOING AND WHAT HE INTENDS TO DO.

(As it is written, I have made thee a father of many nations,) before him whom he believed, even God, who quickeneth the dead, and calleth those things which be not as though they were. Romans 4:17

2. DECREE BLESSING.

There is a life-giving impact when we speak, pray or declare words of blessing over people, situations and ourselves. A blessing does not have to be formal.

It can be spoken in a natural way, for example:

- May you receive God's healing in your body.
- May you experience growth and increase in your business.

We can offer to pray a blessing over a person or situation. We can also incorporate blessing as a tradition, for example, in our family life. Words of blessing will change the atmosphere.

3. OFFER PRAISE AND THANKSGIVING.

Prophetic praise and prayer celebrate what God's has done before it manifests in the Earth realm. Our declarations of praise and thanks shift the atmosphere and contain the power for breakthrough. Miraculous power is released when we decree according to God's purposes in Jesus' name.

4. PRAY AND ASK GOD FOR SPECIFIC SCRIPTURES.

Seek specific scriptures that reflect what God's heart and purpose are, and what He is doing. *Prophetic* means that we have insight from the Holy Spirit and God's Word as to His intended outcome for a situation or for a people. There is tremendous authority in declaring His words.

CHAPTER 12

SOME CONCLUDING THOUGHTS

So what have we learned so far? We have learned:

- That prayer can be specific, targeted and anointed so that it reaches its intended goal with the ability to make things happen.
- That we have, within our own mouths, the ability to change the atmosphere in a given situation.

- That each of us has been created with a specific purpose, and our presence here on earth is intended to change things for the better for all those we touch.
- That we have the ability to declare a thing that we know to be the will of God and see it come to pass.
- That God has called us to put forth a personal manifesto and to live by it and see it fulfilled.
- That we have the right (and the obligation) to stand in the gap for others, even to the point of taking personal responsibility for their sins and shortcomings and seeking God for forgiveness and for change.
- That, as servants of the Most High God, we have authority over false gods.

- That, as servants of the Most High, we are capable of bringing down demon strongholds.
- That as sons of God we have access to all the wisdom of the Almighty.
- That the blood of Christ can do much more than we ever imagined.
- And many other powerful and life-changing truths.

Still, we are just getting started. The companion book, *Learning to Use Your Most Powerful Weapon*, will build and expand on these truths and take us deeper into a life of effective prayer and spiritual warfare. My prayer for you is that you continue growing and learning.

APPENDICES

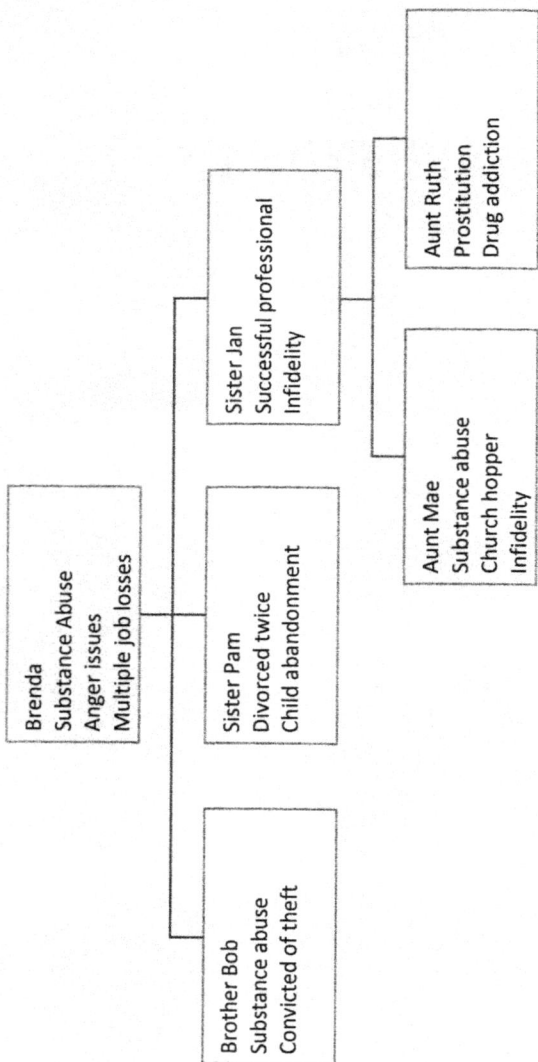

Brenda
Substance Abuse
Anger issues
Multiple job losses

Brother Bob
Substance abuse
Convicted of theft

Sister Pam
Divorced twice
Child abandonment

Sister Jan
Successful professional
Infidelity

Aunt Mae
Substance abuse
Church hopper
Infidelity

Aunt Ruth
Prostitution
Drug addiction

Prayer Mapping

In the sample on the facing page, we can see the following:

There is a clear pattern visible of the issues affecting Brenda. A quick examination indicates that a history has been established through the family linage. You could pray for the immediate symptoms or you could choose to target the prevailing thread that has plagued her family line.

To address substance abuse, you can attack dependence on substances, but often they just cover up reality. A spirit of avoidance is likely to be in operation.

Not being able to keep a job may have its root in infidelity. Use the template on the following page to create your own map.

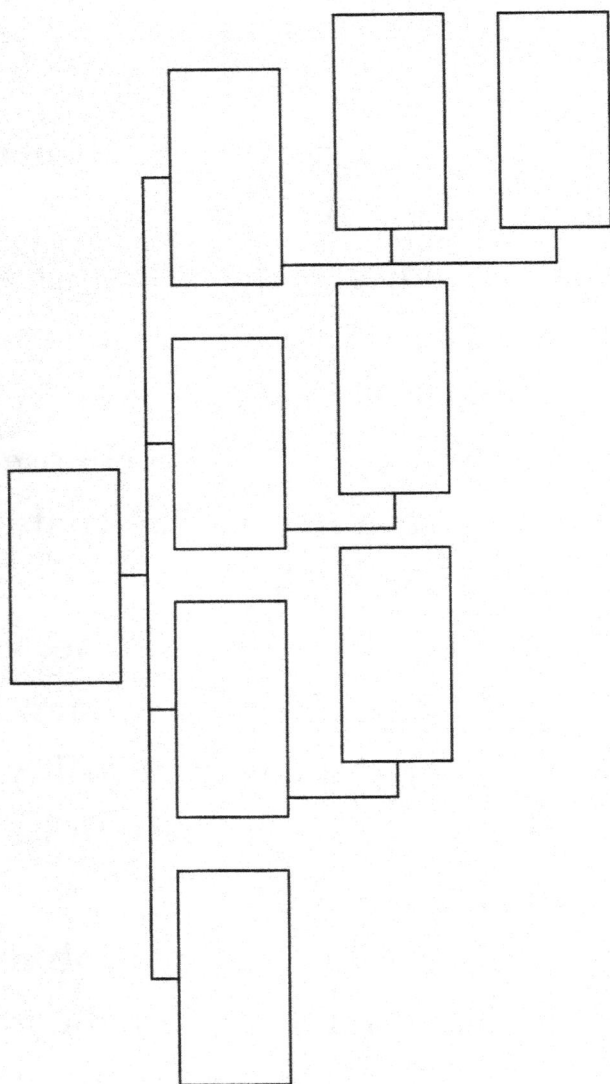

Other Books
by
Prophetess Jackie Harewood

Sing Unto the Lord a New Song: An Introduction to Praise and Worship
(0-97-9712623-0-6)

The Violent Take It by Force
(978-1-934769-11-9)

Intercession Builds Bridges: Frequently Asked Questions About Intercession
(978-1-59872-909-2)

Overshadowed by the Almighty
(978-1-934769-99-7)

Learning to Use Your Greatest Weapon
(978-1-940461-56-4)

The Violent Take it by Force

Intercession Made Easy

Jackie Harewood

Overshadowed by the Almighty

Understanding the Phenomenon Known as "Being Slain in the Spirit"

With a special chapter entitled **What Does God's Voice Sound Like?**

Prophetess Jackie Harewood

Learning

to

Use

Your

Greatest

Weapon

Prophetess Jackie Harewood

I *Will* Bless THEE

Discovering the Untapped Power of COVENANT

Apostle David Harewood

MINISTRY PAGE

Prophetess Jackie Harewood
37041 Agnes Webb Avenue
Prairieville, LA 70769

jharewoodla@cox.net
(225) 772-14552